When Life Gives Us WIND

Written By Florenza Denise Lee

Illustrated By LaTay D. Harris

This Book Belongs To:

_____

When Life Gives Us Wind

Address inquiries to Contact@florenza.org.

eBook ISBN 978-1-941328-22-4
Softcover ISBN 978-1-941328-04-0
Hardcover ISBN 978-1-941328-21-7

LCCN 2020943723

Words to Ponder Publishing Company, LLC
Printed in the United States of America.
For more information, visit https://www.florenza.org.

Published titles by Florenza are:

Adventurous Olivia's Alphabet Quest
Amiri's Birthday Wish
Barry Bear's Very Best, Learning to Say No to Negative Influences
If…The Story of Faith Walker
There's No Place Like My Own Home
The Tail of Max the Mindless Dog, A Children's Book on Mindfulness
Welcome Home Daddy, Love, Lexi
When Life Gives Us Wind

Children's Books coming soon are:

Acornsville, Land of the Secret Seed Keepers
Adventurous Olivia's Numerical Quest
Adventurous Olivia's Garden Surprise
Brooklyn Beaver ALMOST Builds a Dam
Manny & Tutu
Micah and Malik's Super Awesome Excellent Adventure
Mind Your Manners, Mia
Oh, My Goodness, Look at this Big Mess
Two Bees in a Hive

Young Reader Chapter Books coming soon are:

Hoku to the Rescue
Home Is Where the Heart Is
Two-Thirds is a Whole

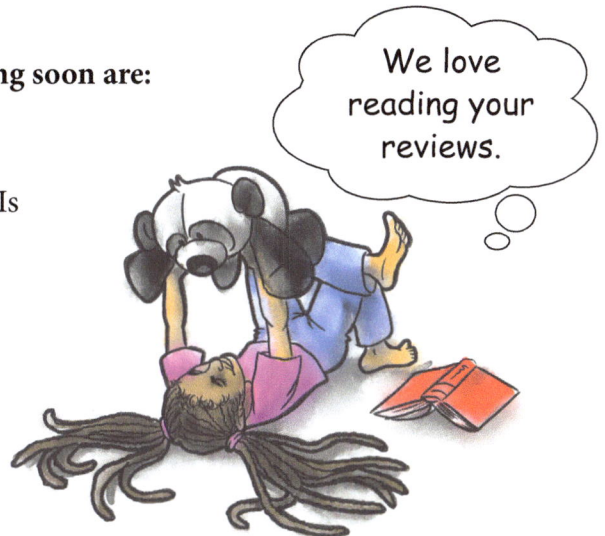

We love reading your reviews.

I want to thank Jessica and Missy, my loudest cheerleaders, and my greatest joy! And, to Papa Bear, my hero! I also dedicate this book to all the small heroes who remain at home while their moms and dads deploy to faraway places. Never forget how loved, missed and respected you are. Although you have never deployed, you are just as brave.

- Florenza

"To all the military babies like me!"

LaTay D. Harris has been an artist all her life, starting with traditional art during early childhood, and expanding her craft throughout her years from drawing and painting to digital art and tattooing. She is mostly self-taught and continues to increase her skill level with every new creation, taking inspiration from her peers and the world around her.

Please follow LaTay at:

www.blvqwulphart.com

www.facebook.com/blvqwulphart

www.instagram.com/blvqwulph

Hi, my name is Xiomara.
Mom calls me Mars.
It's just Mom and me.

Mom wears a uniform and combat boots; she is in the military. I am very proud of her. She defends our country.

I love when my mom receives orders. We have moved eight times. I like meeting new friends, eating different foods, and learning new languages.

I learned that, hello in German is Guten tag. Thank you in Hawaiian is Mahalo. Please, in Spanish, is Por favor. Goodbye in French is Au revoir.

Moving can be scary, but also a lot of fun. Mom says we have to make the best of every situation life gives us. She says very few people experience all that we have; we are very fortunate.

When I am nervous, Mom says, "Mars, when life gives us wind, we have two options ..."

"We may complain," I respond, "or fly kites."

She says it doesn't matter where we live, as long as we are together, we have all that we will ever need.

One day, Mom picks me up from school;
she isn't smiling as much as usual. She looks very serious.
I ask, "Is everything okay?"
"Everything is just fine," she replies as we drive home.

13

Once we are inside and put away our things,
I help prepare dinner. As we eat, I ask about her day.

"Mars, I need to talk to you about something important."

I bite my bottom lip; my heart beats a little faster, and tears begin
to sting my eyes. Mom reaches over and holds my hand,
then pats her leg for me to come on her lap.
She tells me she received orders to deploy.

"Orders? We're moving? Where? When?
How long before the movers come?
I love moving!"

"Mars, you will not be able to go
with me this time."

I don't think I heard Mom correctly.
I am so confused. We have never been apart, not ever.
"Did...did you say that I...I...I...cannot go with you?" I stammer.

Mom explains that deployments are when servicemembers relocate to faraway places; families are not allowed to go.

"If I can't go with you, where will I live?"

She says I will stay with Grandma and Popi. I haven't seen them since I was small.

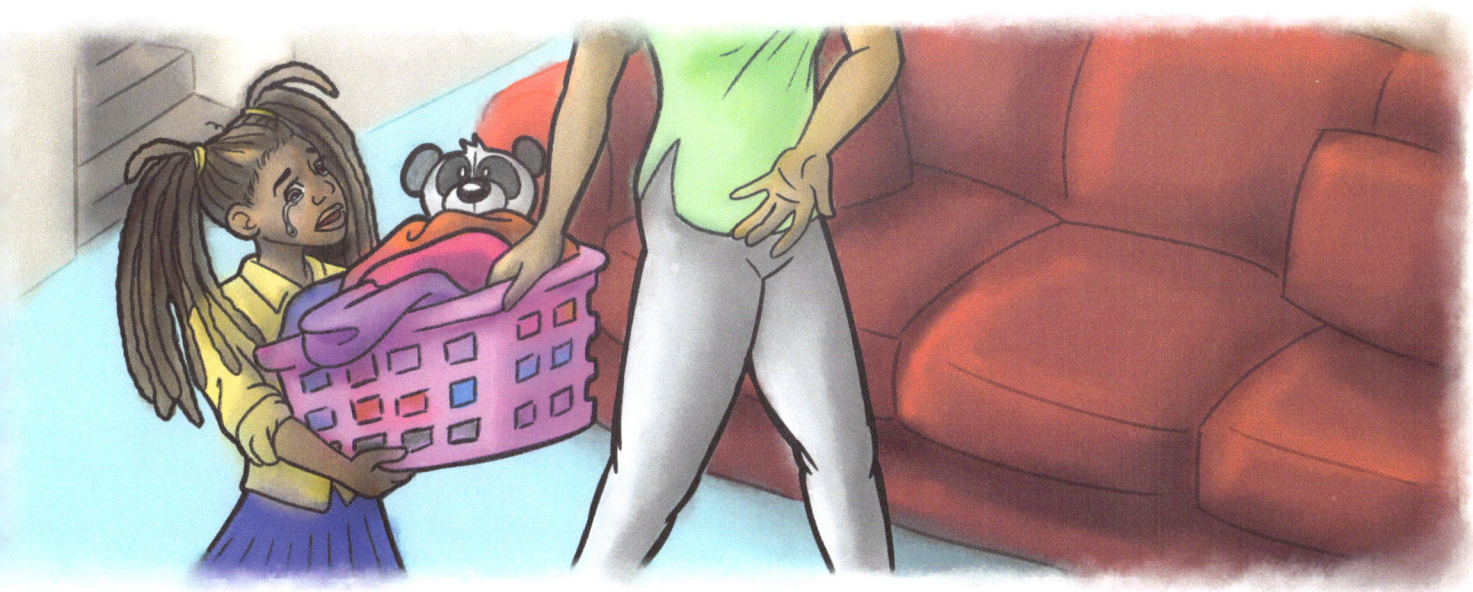

I have never stayed with my grandparents by myself. What if I do not like living with them? What if they don't want me being there?

Mom assures me that it won't be forever.
"Before you know it, I will be back home. When life
gives us wind..." she begins to say.

I open my mouth to respond, but the words will not come out. Inside I am screaming, "WE COMPLAIN, MOMMY, WE COMPLAIN!"

We spend the next few weeks discussing ways we will remain in touch. Mom shows me on the computer where she will be stationed. It looks very far away. She tells me again everything will be just fine.

The time arrives for us to travel to my grandparents. We pack my clothes, toys, and books. As we ride to the airport, she tells me all about her childhood; she smiles as she talks. I love seeing her smile. She has the best laugh ever.

It has been a very long time since I saw my grandparents. I am very nervous. As we board the plane, Mommy tells me again about when she was young, like me, and all the fun times she had with Grandma and Popi as a child. The flight was long; we talked the whole way there.

Grandma and Popi are waiting for us when we arrive. They are so happy to see us. Grandma has baked chocolate chips cookies; they are my favorite. Smelling them makes me forget about being nervous.

Popi takes my things to Mom's old bedroom. Around their house are pictures of her when she was little. Some pictures are hard to tell if they are of Mom, or of me.

Later, Mom helps me get settled into her old room. She talks about all her childhood memories. She laughs as she tells me the names of her stuffed animals and the people in the pictures on the walls.
I giggle when I see them.

When it is time for Mom to leave, I begin to cry. She says she loves me, and for me to have fun.
We all give her hugs and kisses.

After supper, Grandma shows me more pictures of Mom growing up. Some are funny, others are beautiful, and all are of my mom. When it is time for bed, they come into the room to say goodnight.

Popi sees my book and says, "Mars, this was your mom's favorite book; may I read it to you before you go to sleep?"

I say yes, right away!

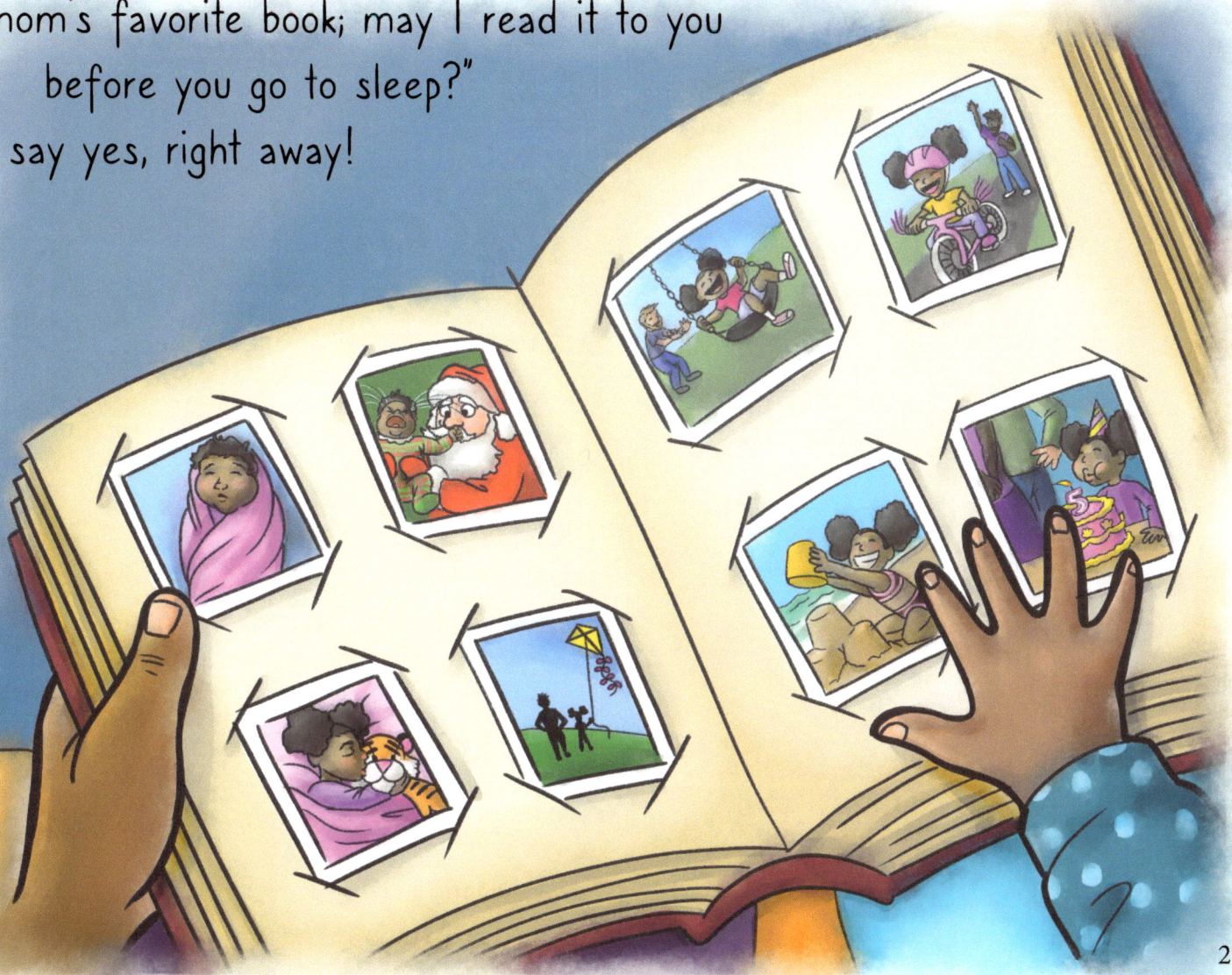

Popi uses funny voices as he reads. He knows all the parts by heart. Grandma and I giggle as he speaks.

After he reads the book, Popi says he is happy I am staying with them. Grandma says she is very happy too. Both of them give me a big hug, and say good night.

As they are leaving, I smile and hug Panda.
I am going to miss Mommy, but I am also going to
love staying with my grandparents.

"When life gives us wind..." I whisper to Panda as they
turn off the lights to leave.
"We may complain," answers Popi,
"Or fly kites," giggles Grandma.

I close my eyes, and go to sleep. Mom was right.
I am going to be just fine.

The End

www.ingramcontent.com/pod-product-compliance
Lightning Source LLC
LaVergne TN
LVHW072115070426
835510LV00002B/64